BRANCH LINES
TO HORSHAM

First published 1982.

ISBN 0 906520 02 9

© *Middleton Press, 1982*

Published by   Middleton Press
Easebourne Lane
Midhurst, West Sussex.
GU29 9AZ

Printed & bound by   Biddles Ltd.,
Guildford and Kings Lynn.

Maps

Except where otherwise stated, the scale is 25″ to 1 mile but the following initial letters apply throughout.

BM   Bench Mark
Cr   Crane
MP   Mile Post
SB   Signal Box
SP   Signal Post

Index

Authors' Notes

It seems that most people consider railways to consist of main lines and branch lines. The lines featured in this book were certainly never regarded as main lines – secondary lines maybe – but they always had the atmosphere and down-rated rolling stock of the branch line. The L.B.S.C.R. always described the Cranleigh route as its "Guildford Branch" and British Railways issued tickets for the centenary of its "Steyning Branch". Moreover, neither line has shown more than one through train a day for over forty years. The title "Branch Lines to Horsham" therefore seemed apt and as they both had a century of steam traction, the iron horse predominates in this album.

From the intimacy of the narrow Wey gap in the North Downs, through the broad views of the Wealden landscape, to the relatively wide, uncluttered Adur gap in the South Downs, the railway traveller was not distracted from the rural scene as even the marshalling yards were to the north of both Guildford and Horsham. The various country stations displayed their cluster of sidings, the inevitable goods shed and, here and there, some signs of mineral working. We have endeavoured to select photographs which show these cross-country rail routes in the life and scenery of this district as well as for their pure railway interest.

Acknowledgements

We would like to record our appreciation of the help received from the photographers named in the captions, and also from G. Birdfield, P. Clark, T. Clark (station signs), M. J. Grainger, R. H. R. Harmer, L. James, S. G. Peto, and N. Stanyon. The work of the late E. Wallis is reproduced by the kind permission of Mrs. Wallis and with the untiring help of David Wallis. The route maps in the introduction are by courtesy of the editor of the Railway Magazine. As ever, our wives have been tolerant, encouraging and helpful for which we are very grateful.

Publisher's Notes

We were grateful for the enthusiastic reception of our first Railway Album "Branch Lines to Midhurst" and have therefore used a similar format and paper for this publication. The high quality matt paper gives full detail to the pictures without the need to adjust the book position to eliminate reflected light.

GEOGRAPHICAL SETTING

Guildford to Horsham

Guildford is situated in a natural gap in the North Downs through which the River Wey flows northwards to the Thames. Immediately to the south of the station, the chalk of the North Downs was extensively excavated to accommodate the locomotive round-house, the site now being the station car park. Continuing southwards, the chalk hills are penetrated by a tunnel 833 yards long for the L.S.W.R. main line to Portsmouth, and within a ¼ mile another tunnel pierces the upper greensand of St. Catherine's Hill. When built, this was 133 yards long, but was extended northwards in 1981 because of frequent landslips, also a problem when the tunnel was constructed.

Shortly after leaving this tunnel, there is a fine view of the River Wey and a little over one mile from Guildford the double track line to Dorking and Redhill branches off to the east at Shalford Junction.

Peasmarsh Junction was formerly about ½ mile further on and trains left the main line here to join the L.B.S.C.R. single track route to Horsham. After crossing the River Wey, which is still navigable as far as Godalming, the line ran close to a tributary of this river for many miles. At one time this was also used by canal boats and formed part of an inland link between London and Portsmouth, closing soon after the advent of the railway.

A steady climb through Bramley and Cranleigh took the trains to 250 ft. above sea level at the summit in Baynards Tunnel. This marked the water shed between the Wey and Arun, the boundary between Surrey and Sussex and also the Western and Central sections of the Southern Region of British Railways. Falling gradients for 1½ miles took the traveller through Rudgwick to the bridge over the River Arun, followed by a short climb up to Slinfold. A couple of miles of fairly level running reached the junction with the Mid-Sussex line at Christs Hospital. All regular trains ran on to Horsham, a further 2½ miles.

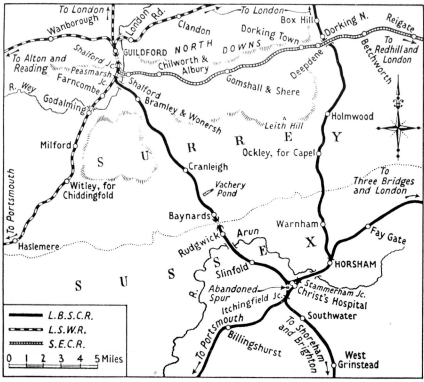

Map of the railways in the Horsham and Guildford areas, showing pre-grouping ownership

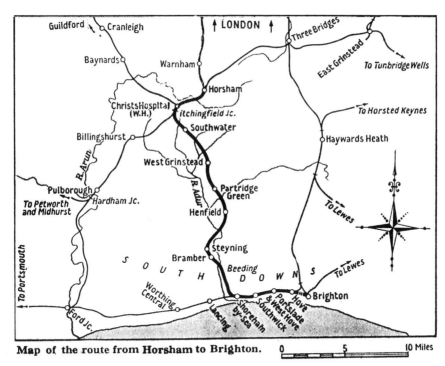

Map of the route from **Horsham** to **Brighton**.   0   5   10 Miles

Horsham to Shoreham

This double track route branched from the Mid-Sussex line at Itchingfield Junction, nearly a mile south of Christs Hospital. The claypits at Southwater brickworks expose to view the Wealden clay over which the railway runs from Bramley to Henfield. This gives rise to a fairly uniform and gently undulating landscape with extensive pasture land interspersed with coppices.

After leaving the market town of Steyning, the line passes the remains of Bramber Castle which once defended the natural gap in the South Downs containing the River Adur. The line crosses the river no less than three times. Running along the tidal reach of the river, there were three memorable features on this journey. Firstly Lancing College perched high on the cut end of the Downs, its impressive chapel silhouetted against the sky. Secondly, Beeding Cement Works placed functionally on the opposite cut end revealing its giant scar in the chalk. Thirdly, the frail wooden road bridge, linking the divided coastal plain, at the end of which the signalmen apparently issued tickets to passing motorists. In reality the railway owned the bridge and collected tolls at the level crossing before the present concrete structure strode across the valley, spreading spaghetti on the eastern shore.

Historical Background

A branch from the London to Southampton Railway reached Guildford in 1845 and was extended by the L.S.W.R. to Godalming in 1849 and to Havant in 1859. The Guildford traffic was much sought after and the South Eastern Railway reached the town via Dorking in 1849, but it was not until 2nd October, 1865, that the L.B.S.C.R. arrived with its branch from Horsham.

The Horsham and Guildford Direct Railway was an independent company authorised to construct the line in 1860. Initially the Board were in favour of the L.S.W.R. operating the railway, but with changes of directors the policy was reversed and the L.B.S.C.R. took over the company before construction was complete.

Horsham was reached by a branch from Three Bridges on the London to Brighton line in 1848, although a Railway Hotel had been opened by an optimist 12 years earlier. The L.B.S.C.R. extended this branch to Petworth, of all places, in 1859 (more optimists), today's main line through Arundel not opening until 1863.

Railway development in Sussex started on the coast in 1840 with the opening of the Shoreham to Brighton line, which facilitated the building of the London line as materials could come by sea to Shoreham harbour and construction could proceed from both ends. The L.B.S.C.R. had been authorised by Parliament to build a line between Shoreham and Horsham in 1858. It was opened in 1861; on July 1st south of Partridge Green and the remainder on September 16th. The line was single initially being doubled around 1880, and was often used as a diversionary route when the main line between Brighton and London was blocked, as it was in August, 1861, by a collision in Clayton tunnel.

The entire Guildford to Shoreham route was listed for closure in the Beeching Plan, the last regular trains running on the Cranleigh line on June 12th, 1965, and the Steyning portion on March 5th, 1966, most freight services having been withdrawn in 1962-3.

The L.C.G.B. ran a special train between Horsham and Guildford on Sunday June 13th, but the final movements were made on the following day, when wagons were removed from Baynards to Horsham.

On the Steyning line, the last train was a van train which was run during the early hours of Sunday March 6th to collect furniture from the station. It left Bramber at 00.10 and called at all stations, the last stop being at Southwater at 3.20am.

An unsuccessful attempt to operate the Cranleigh line privately was made in the months after closure but it was not until 1981 that a scheme was launched to save part of the Steyning route. Following cessation of trains to the Cement Works from Shoreham, Mr. Peter Cannon of Upper Beeding formed the Southern Railway Preservation Society, whose objective is to save the remaining length of single track for steam operation.

ACCIDENTS AND AIR ATTACKS

On 11th August, 1866, the 7.40 pm fast train from London Bridge to Portsmouth overran the signals at Itchingfield Junction and collided with the locomotive and leading brakevan of an up train from Shoreham. The fireman of the down train died but there were no other injuries.

Two other incidents of German aircraft attacking trains have been recorded. On 30th November, 1942, a Class C3 locomotive no. 2308 was hauling a goods train mainly of conflat wagons from Horsham to Steyning when it was attacked near West Grinstead. The driver received fatal injuries. A German Dornier 217 machine gunned and bombed a passenger train near Bramley on 16th December, 1942. It was a two-coach train loaded with Christmas shoppers. Seven people were killed, including the driver and guard.

Bramley was the scene of a later accident in which a train departed with the points wrongly set and accelerated into the buffers. This was caused by a combination of factors. Firstly, the weather was bad and trains were running late and, secondly, the electric staff was out of action between Peasmarsh and Bramley and pilot working was in force. Because of late running, it was necessary to cross two trains at Bramley, an unusual occurrence. The up train arrived first, but the signalman omitted to change the road behind it. Regulation 25 of the BR Rule Book states that if the staff is out of action, the signal allowing entrance to a section should not be pulled off, but kept on and the driver warned. As a result, the failure to change the road was not discovered, as it would have been if any attempt to pull off the signal had been made, and the down train ran in the darkness off into the shunting neck and had attained considerable speed before colliding with the buffer stops.

History repeated itself on 5th March, 1964, when two trains collided at Itchingfield Junction due to one train overrunning the signals. This event is described and illustrated elsewhere in this book.

PASSENGER TRAIN SERVICES

The Cranleigh line on opening was provided with four trains each way (reduced to three within four years) and two on Sundays, all having 1st, 2nd and 3rd class compartments in the loose coupled 4-wheeled coaches. In late Victorian times, up to six complete trips were made with one or two extra trains from Horsham terminating at Cranleigh. Gradually the number of classes was reduced to one (3rd) and the number of trains increased to eight. Every train stopped at all stations and there was seldom any through working of passenger trains to other lines, the notable exception being excursions, particularly on Sundays, often from the West Midlands to Brighton. This necessitated reversal at Christs Hospital, but in later years this was often done at Horsham as the locomotive depot was located there, and a change of engines was usually made. It also avoided blocking the main line as Horsham has four through platform roads. In the 1930s a late evening trip between Guildford and Cranleigh was operated on Wednesdays and Saturdays mainly for the benefit of cinema patrons. A similar short journey was run in the last years of the line in the early evening, principally for season ticket holders.

The Steyning line was initially provided with five trains each way with one continuing to Three Bridges. Almost all trains on this route throughout its life started or finished their journeys at Brighton and called at all stations. The service increased gradually to eleven journeys in each direction after the electrification of the Arundel line in 1938. Until that time a number of trains were worked to and from London but thereafter there was one departure only from the capital city and that was soon after 5 am. It usually included a fish van with overnight deliveries from Grimsby. Between the Wars, an additional train was run between Steyning and Brighton for business people (before "commuters" were invented) and for many years the train was kept overnight at Steyning. 1958 saw the introduction of a regular hourly service (two hourly on Sundays) but this improvement was not sufficient to prevent closure. Excursion traffic was received not only via the Cranleigh line but from various South London stations during the summer, but this traffic declined after 1960.

Station Master Bartlett was resident at West Grinstead from 1958 and cared for all the stations on the branch. He is seen here locking Steyning station after the departure of the final passenger train.
(Shoreham Herald)

LOCOMOTIVES

The L.B.S.C.R. locomotive engineer, John Craven, produced one small tank engine of 2-2-2 wheel arrangement at Brighton Works in 1865 for use on the company's Guildford branch, where it worked for 21 years.

Terriers No. 36 "Bramley" and No. 77 "Wonersh" ran on the Cranleigh line from Bramley shed until it was closed, after which they were operated from the L.S.W.R. shed at Guildford, being maintained at Horsham on Sundays. They were sent new to the line in 1878 and 1880 respectively. "Wonersh" was sent away in the nineties to work the Pulborough-Chichester line via Midhurst and subsequently was transferred to the Isle of Wight, where it became Southern No. W13 "Carisbrooke". It returned to the mainland in 1949 to become B.R. No. 32677, being based at Fratton until withdrawal in September, 1959. By 1922, it had already travelled over 1.2 million miles! "Bramley" was sold in 1902 to a contractor who was building the Great Central Railway extension.

Stroudley's Belgravia class 2-4-0 tender engines were commonly used on trains between London and Brighton via Horsham in the 1880s. No. 206 "Carisbrooke" was a regular but poor performer on the line.

In the mid 1890s, Class E1 Nos. 97 "Honfleur" and 127 "Poitiers" from Horsham shed shared the local shunting duties and the daily freight service to Guildford.

At the same time there was one regular working of the famous Gladstone class of locomotive via Steyning. This class was a prestigious batch of 0-4-2 tender engines, normally used on the expresses, but once a day one of them travelled a circuit from Brighton via Horsham, Three Bridges, East Grinstead and Tunbridge Wells.

Following World War I, the Gladstones were regularly used on the Steyning line for passenger trains, together with E1, E3 and E5 tanks. Excursion trains after the grouping were hauled variously by the Gladstone, B2X, E5 and ex-SECR F1 classes whilst regular passenger services employed mainly D tanks with some visits by E3, B2X and I3 locomotives.

A larger version of the C2 was the C3 and in 1930 Horsham shed was allocated six of these engines and, although intended for goods trains, they were often used on Sunday excursions to Brighton, taking over a train from Cranleigh line and running it via Steyning.

The D1 0-4-2 tanks nos. 2235 and 2283 were still running to Guildford and Brighton from Horsham during World War II despite both having been built around 1880. Another D1 no. 2252 was seen at Bramber as late as 1950.

Another Billinton design to be used on these lines was the C2 0-6-0 tender freight locomotive. For example, no. 2436 was stationed at Guildford from March, 1944, to work goods on the Cranleigh line. A rebuilt member of this class, C2X B.R. No. 32522, is shown in our previous album "Branch Lines to Midhurst" hauling the last goods train to that town from Chichester. The journey ended spectacularly and ignominiously at the bottom of a stream. No. 32523, another C2X, regularly worked the 9.02 am Hove-Beeding-Horsham-Three Bridges goods until 1962.

Other former L.B.S.C.R. locomotives to work passenger trains on the Cranleigh line were members of the E4 class of 0-6-2 tanks, one of which, "Birchgrove", survives on the Bluebell Railway today. As late as 1962, nos. 32479 and 32503 were used as substitutes for the usual Class 2 standard BR 2-6-2 tank.

In 1954, the last remaining Class D3 0-4-4 tank (No. 32390) was used regularly between Brighton and Horsham, sometimes running on to Guildford. This locomotive had covered over 1.4 million miles since it was built at Brighton in 1894. Other members of this class were regularly used on both lines in earlier years.

Following the formation of the Southern Railway in 1923, former L.S.W.R. 0-4-4 M7 tanks were introduced on the Cranleigh route, not to be ousted until after nationalisation by the introduction of the BR standard Class 2 tanks. Nos. 30047-53 were based at Horsham, but occasionally an E6 appeared. Guildford shed sent out the most unexpected engines from time to time – Classes C, D, Q1 and 700 for example – particularly for the local run to Cranleigh.

The versatile BR Class 2 2-6-2 tanks were used until the end of services on the Cranleigh line and until the introduction of diesel electric multiple units on the Steyning line on May 4th, 1964.

GUILDFORD and HORSHAM

Miles	Down	Week Days a.m		a.m	a.m		p.m SO	p.m		p.m		p.m		p.m SX		p.m	p.m			Sundays a.m		p.m			
	394 London (W.) dep	6A55	..	8ⒶJ12	9 45	..	12 15	12 45	..	4Z20	..	5b20	..	5 45	..	6 45	7 45	..	..	7 25	..	6 27	..	..	..
—	Guildford dep	8 5	..	9 18	10 34	..	1 9	1 42	..	5 4	..	6 7	..	6 34	..	7 34	8 34	..	..	8 54	..	7 22	..	..	..
3½	Bramley and Wonersh	8 12	..	9 30	10 41	..	1 16	1 50	..	5 12	..	6 15	..	6 41	..	7 41	8 42	..	..	9 2	..	7 29	..	..	..
8½	Cranleigh	8 23	..	9 40	10 51	..	1 30	2 1	..	5 22	..	6 26	..	6 51	..	7 51	8 52	..	..	9 12	..	7 39	..	..	..
11½	Baynards	8 32	..	9y51	10 58	..	..	2 10	..	5 30	..	6 37	..	..	..	7 58	9 1	..	..	9 20	..	7 46	..	..	..
12½	Rudgwick	8 36	..	9 55	11 1	..	..	2 14	..	5 33	..	6 41	..	..	..	8 1	9 5	..	..	9 24	..	7 50	..	..	..
14½	Slinfold	8 42	..	10 0	11 7	..	..	2 19	..	5 39	..	6 46	..	..	..	8 7	9 11	..	..	9 30	..	7 55	..	..	..
17½	Christ's Hospital K 159, 244	8 49	..	10y11	11 15	..	..	2 26	..	5 45	..	6 55	..	..	..	8 13	9 19	..	..	9 37	..	8 1	..	..	..
41	244 Brighton arr	..	..	11 26	12 28	..	..	4 26	..	7c29	..	8 25	..	..	..	9 26	..	..	..	..	..	9 23	..	..	..
19½	Horsham 198 arr	8 54	..	10 16	11 22	..	..	2 31	..	5 50	..	7 0	..	..	..	8 18	9 25	..	..	9 43	..	8 7	..	..	..
57	427 London Bridge arr	9‡57	..	11Ⓐ39	..	..	..	..	..	..	..	8Ⓐ38	..	..	..	9Ⓐ38	11Ⓐ11	..	..	11Ⓐ10	..	10 7	..	..	..
57	427 Victoria "	10Ⓐ13	..	11 32	12 40	..	..	3 40	..	7Ⓐ13	..	8 40	..	..	..	9 40	11 7	..	..	11 6	..	9 40	..	..	..

Miles	Up	Week Days a.m	a.m	a.m	a.m	a.m		p.m SO	p.m SX	p.m SO		p.m	p.m SO	p.m SX		p.m SX		p.m			Sundays a.m		p.m			
	394 Victoria dep	..	..	6Ⓐ15	7 47	11 18	..	..	1 48	2 18	..	3 18	4Ⓐ26	5 4	..	..	..	6U18	..	..	9 18	..	7 19	..	..	..
	394 London Bridge "	..	..	6Ⓐ28	8Ⓐ10	..	..	..	1Ⓐ31	2Ⓐ8	..	3Ⓐ25	4Ⓐ28	5 15	..	..	..	5U48	..	..	8Ⓐ55	..	6Ⓐ55	..	..	..
—	Horsham dep	6 36	..	7 59	9 30	12 22	..	..	3 23	3 23	..	4 53	6 0	6 18	..	..	..	7 12	..	..	10 19	..	8 23	..	..	..
—	244 Brighton dep	..	..	6 30	8 0	9 30	..	..	2 0	1 35	..	3 57	4 58	4 58	..	..	..	6V15	..	..	7 23	..	6 25	..	..	..
2½	Christ's Hospital, West Horsham	..	..	8 3	9 35	12 26	..	..	3 27	3 27	..	4 58	6 4	6 22	..	..	..	7 16	..	..	10 23	..	8 27	..	..	..
4½	Slinfold	..	..	8 9	9 41	12 32	..	..	3 33	3 33	..	5 4	6 10	6 28	..	..	..	7 22	..	..	10 29	..	8 32	..	..	..
7	Rudgwick	6 51	..	8 13	9 45	12 37	..	..	3 37	3 37	..	5 10	6 15	6 33	..	..	..	7 26	..	..	10 33	..	8 37	..	..	..
8½	Baynards	6 57	..	8 17	9 49	12 42	..	..	3 41	3 41	..	5 14	6 20	6 37	..	..	..	7 30	..	..	10 37	..	8 40	..	..	..
11½	Cranleigh	7 5	7 18	8 24	9 56	12 49	..	1 46	3 48	3 48	..	5 21	6 27	6L52	..	7 19	..	7T54	..	..	10 43	..	8 46	..	..	..
16½	Bramley and Wonersh	..	7 27	8 36	10 6	12 59	..	1 50	3 58	3 58	..	5 35	6 39	7 5	..	7 28	..	8 5	..	..	10 53	..	8 56	..	..	..
19½	Guildford 246, 249, 359, 427 arr	..	7 36	8 45	10 14	1 7	..	2 1	4 6	4 6	..	5 47	6 51	7 13	..	7 36	..	8 13	..	..	11 1	..	9 4	..	..	..
50	427 London (W.) arr	..	8 29	9 30	11 2	2 1	..	3 1	5 3	5 3	..	6 46	8 3	8 3	..	8 46	..	9 3	..	..	12 1	..	10 1	..	..	..

Ⓐ Third class only
‡ 8 minutes later on Saturdays

A Depart 7 15 a.m. on Saturdays
§ 3 minutes later on Saturdays
b Depart 5 15 p.m. on Saturdays

c 3 minutes *earlier* on Saturdays
J Dep. 8 15 a.m. on Saturdays, 1st and 3rd class
K Christ's Hospital, West Horsham
L Arr. 6 44 p.m.

SO or S0 Saturdays only
SX Saturdays excepted
T Arr. 7 36 p.m.
U Dep. Victoria 5 48 and London Bridge 5Ⓐ31 p.m. on Saturdays
V Dep. 5 55 p.m. on Saturdays

y Arr. 5 minutes *earlier*
Z Dep. 4 15 p.m. on Saturdays

OTHER TRAINS BETWEEN Christ's Hospital and Horsham — PAGES 196 and 244

Summer 1948 timetable.

HORSHAM, SHOREHAM-BY-SEA, and BRIGHTON

Miles	Down	Week Days a.m	a.m	a.m	a.m	a.m SX	a.m SO	p.m WO	p.m SX	p.m SO	p.m SX	p.m SO	p.m	p.m SO	p.m SX	p.m SO	p.m SX	p.m SO	p.m SX	p.m	Sundays a.m	a.m		p.m	p.m	p.m
	394 Victoria dep	..	5*20	6 40	9 18	10 18	10 18	..	12 18	12 18	1 48	2 18	3 18	4 18	4 18	5 18	5 30	5 48	6 18	7 18	6 40	7 46	..	12 48	3 18	7 18
	394 London Bridge "	..	5 25	6Ⓐ35	9Ⓐ15	10Ⓐ8	10Ⓐ8	..	12 18	12*15	1Ⓐ31	2Ⓐ8	..	..	4Ⓐ7	..	5 15	5Ⓐ31	5 48	..	..	7Ⓐ55	..	..	2Ⓐ5	6Ⓐ55
	394 Waterloo "	..	..	6Ⓐ27	9Ⓐ7	9Ⓐ47	9Ⓐ47	..	12Ⓐ7	12Ⓐ7	..	2Ⓐ7	2Ⓐ3027	4Ⓐ7	4Ⓐ7	5Ⓐ7	5Ⓐ7	..	6Ⓐ7	..	..	8Ⓐ2	..	12Ⓐ42	2Ⓐ42	7Ⓐ2
—	Horsham dep	..	7 14	8 12	10 23	11 19	11 25	..	1 39		3 19		4 19	5 19		6 19	6 25	7 19		8 19	8 19	9 19	..	2 40	4 19	8 19
2½	Christ's Hospital K	..	7 21	8 16	10 27	11 23	11 29	..	1 43		3 23		4 23	5 23		6 23	6 29	7 23		8 23	8 23	9 23	..	2 44	4 23	8 23
4½	Southwater	..	7 27	8 22	10 32	11 29	11 35	..	1 48		3 29		4 29	5 29		6 29	6 35	7 29		8 29	8 29	9 29	..	2 49	4 29	8 29
7	West Grinstead	..	7 35	8 29	10 39	11 37	11 42	..	1 55		3 36		4 36	5 36		6 36	6 42	7 36		8 36	8 36	9 36	..	2 56	4 36	8 36
9½	Partridge Green	..	7 41	8 36	10 45	11 43	11 48	..	2 1		3 43		4 43	5 43		6 43	6 48	7 43		8 43	8 43	9 43	..	3 2	4 43	8 42
11½	Henfield	..	7 46	8 41	10 50	11 49	11 53	..	2 5		3 48		4 48	5 48		6 48	6 53	7 48		8 48	8 48	9 48	..	3 7	4 48	8 47
15½	Steyning	7 40	7 56	8 50	10 58	11 58	12 1	12 16	2 14		3 56		4 57	5 58		6 56	7 1	7 56		8 56	8 57	9 57	..	3 16	4 57	8 56
16	Bramber	7 42	7 59	8 54	11 2	12 2	12 4	12 13	2 18		4 0		5 1	6 1		6 59	7 4	7 59		8 59	9 0	10 0	..	3 19	5 0	8 59
20	Shoreham-by-Sea J 158	7 51	8 10	9 6	11 12	12 11	12 11	12 27	2 28		4 9		5 11	6 11		7 9	7 13	8 9		9 8	9 9	10 9	..	3 28	5 10	9 9
21½	Southwick	7 55	..	9 9	..	..	..	..	2 32		4 13		..	6 16		7 12	..	8 12		9 12	9 13	10 13	..	..	..	..
23	Portslade and West Hove	7 58	8 16	9 13	11 17	12 17	12 17	..	..		4 17		5 16	6 19		7 17	7 19	8 16		9 16	9 16	10 18	..	..	5 16	..
24½	Hove	8 2	8 19	9 17	11 21	12 21	12 21	12 35	2 38		4 21		5 20	6 23		7 21	7 24	8 20		9 21	9 20	10 22	..	3 36	5 20	9 18
26	Brighton 158, 197, 239 arr	8 7	8 24	9 22	11 26	12 26	12 28	12 40	2 43		4 26		5 25	6 28		7 26	7 29	8 25		9 26	9 25	10 27	..	3 41	5 25	9 23

Miles	Up	Week Days a.m	a.m	a.m	a.m WO		p.m	p.m SO	p.m SX	p.m	p.m	p.m SO		p.m SX		p.m	p.m	p.m		Sundays a.m	a.m		p.m	p.m	p.m
—	Brighton dep	6 30	8 0	9 30	11 20	..	12 12	1 35	2 0	3 57	4 58	5 55	..	6 15	..	7 15	8 12	9 57	..	7 23	10 7	..	2 25	6 25	8 55
1½	Hove	6 34	8 4	9 34	11 23	..	12 16	1 39	2 4	4 1	5 2	5 59	..	6 20	..	7 19	8 16	10 1	..	7 28	10 12	..	2 29	6 29	8 59
3	Portslade and West Hove	6 38	8 8	9 38	11 28	..	..	1 42	2 8	4 4	5 5	..	..	6 23	..	7 22	..	10 5	..	7 32	10 16	..	2 33	6 33	9 3
4½	Southwick	6 42	8 12	..	11 31	..	..	..	..	4 8	5 9	..	..	6 27	..	..	..	10 8	..	7 36	10 20	..	2 37	6 37	9 7
6	Shoreham-by-Sea J	6 46	8 16	9 44	11 46	..	12 24	1 48	2 13	4 12	5 12	6 8	..	6 30	..	7 28	8 24	10 12	..	7 40	10 24	..	2 41	6 41	9 11
10	Bramber	6 55	8 25	9 53	11 54	..	12 32	1 56	2 22	4 20	5 21	6 17	..	6 39	..	7 37	8 33	10 21	..	7 49	10 33	..	2 50	6 50	9 20
10½	Steyning	6 59	8 30	9 56	11 57	..	12 36	1 59	2 25	4 24	5 25	6 20	..	6 42	..	7 41	8 38	10 24	..	7 53	10 38	..	2 54	6 54	9 24
14½	Henfield	7 7	8 39	10 3	..	..	12 44	2 7	2 33	4 32	5 33	6 28	..	6 50	..	7 50	8 45	..	..	8 1	10 46	..	3 1	7 2	9 32
16½	Partridge Green	7 13	8 45	10 8	..	..	12 49	2 12	2 38	4 37	5 38	6 33	..	6 55	..	7 56	8 55	..	..	8 7	10 55	..	3 6	7 7	9 37
18½	West Grinstead	7 20	8 52	10 14	..	..	12 55	2 17	2 44	4 42	5 44	6 39	..	7 0	..	8 3	9 2	..	..	8 13	11 2	..	3 12	7 14	9 43
21½	Southwater	7 28	8 59	10 21	..	..	1 2	2 24	2 51	4 49	5 50	6 45	..	7 7	..	8 10	9 9	..	..	8 20	11 10	..	3 18	7 21	9 50
23½	Christ's Hospital K 159, 245	7 33	9 6	10 26	..	..	1 10	2 29	2 57	4 54	5 56	6 51	..	7 13	..	8 17	9 14	..	..	8 25	11 16	..	3 23	7 27	9 55
26	Horsham 196 arr	7 38	9 14	10 31	..	..	1 16	2 34	3 1	5 0	6 3	6 56	..	7 18	..	8 23	9 19	..	..	8 30	11 21	..	3 28	7 32	10 0
61½	427 Waterloo arr	9Ⓐ4	10ⒶSO43	12Ⓐ3	..	..	2Ⓐ42	4Ⓐ3	4Ⓐ43	3ⒶSX43	7ⒶV43	9Ⓐ3	..	9Ⓐ3	..	10Ⓐ3	11Ⓐ3	..	..	9Ⓐ50	12Ⓐ59	..	4Ⓐ59	8Ⓐ59	12Ⓐ6
62	427 London Bridge "	8*43	10*40	..	..	..	2ⒶA38	..	4 36	6 36	7ⒶL44	8Ⓐ38	..	8Ⓐ38	..	10Ⓐ11	10Ⓐ40	..	..	9Ⓐ40	1Ⓐ10	..	5Ⓐ10	9Ⓐ4	..
63	427 Victoria "	8 37	10 31	11 22	..	..	2ⒶY50	3 40	..	6 40	7Ⓐ45	8 40	..	8 40	..	9 40	10Ⓐ44	..	..	9 31	1 6	..	5 7	8 43	..

Ⓐ Third class only
* Change at East Croydon
A 7 minutes later on Saturdays
J Station for Lancing College (2 miles)

K Christ's Hospital, West Horsham
L 5 minutes *earlier* on Saturdays
SO or S0 Saturdays only
SX or SX Saturdays excepted

V Arrive 8Ⓐ3 p.m. on Saturdays
WO Wednesdays only
Y Arrive 2 40 p.m. on Saturdays. 1st and 3rd class

For **LOCAL TRAINS** and **intermediate Halts** between Shoreham-by-Sea and Brighton, see page 196.
For **OTHER TRAINS** between Horsham and Christ's Hospital, see pages 159 and 245.

GUILDFORD

Guildford Park Brick Works

Kiln

Kiln

Kiln

S.P.

Cr.

Laundry

Corporation Depôt

RUPERT ROAD

S.Ps.

Goods Shed

L.B.

GUILDFORD PARK ROAD

Cattle Pens

S.P.

Goods Shed

Station

Printing Works

RAILWAY ESPLANADE

River

DENZIL ROAD

GENYN ROAD

P.O.

P.O. ROAD

S.P.

Cr.

S.P.

Cr.

Hotel

Hotel

SURREY HOSPITAL

UPPERTON ROAD

P.D.

FARNHAM ROAD

TESTARD ROAD

Engine Shed

S.B.

F.P.

P.H.

S.P.

MOUN

WHERWELL ROAD

Some interesting points to note on this map of 1916 are the absence of a bay for Effingham Junction line trains, the shape of the engine shed and the presence of a siding to the brickworks.

1. An Edwardian view of a train arriving from London, as seen from the Farnham Road bridge. Below the horse box in the siding on the right is a wagon turntable which is also shown on the map. In the foreground between the rails there is an inspection pit which could be used by engine crews to inspect or lubricate the motion of inside cylindered locomotives whilst the train was standing in the station. (Pamlin Prints)

2. A Class D 0-4-2 tank propelling a train under the Farnham Road bridge on its journey to Horsham on 16th February 1929. The driver was at the controls at the far end of the train leaving the fireman alone on the engine. These were called either motor trains or push-pulls. (H. C. Casserley)

3. Former LBSCR Class D1 No.2252 arriving at Guildford on 3rd September 1932 with a train from Horsham, which includes a 4-wheeled van. The tunnel had been shortened here to allow the construction of the locomotive shed seen on the right. The end of the tunnel lining can be seen before the portal was built and in the siding is ex-LSWR Class G6 No.266. The signal by the telegraph pole was the "tunnel occupied indicator" and showed a black spot when shunting was prohibited. (H. C. Casserley)

5. The locomotive round house viewed from the Farnham Road bridge on 30th May 1961, showing a Class 700 on the turntable and the shed pilot Class B4 0-4-0T No.30089 on the right, shortly before the end of its life of over 60 years. The Class E4 0-6-2T in the foreground is seen arriving with the Horsham train at 10.14 a.m. (R. S. Greenwood)

4. There appears to be a predominance of horse drawn traffic in this view of the station approach, taken in the 1930s. Drovers moving cattle between the goods yard and the market sometimes had problems here, as the animals could bolt in different directions at this road junction.　(N. Hamshere)

6. Three weeks later a member of the same class comes into the sunlight briefly between the two tunnels south of Guildford, hauling the 10.34 a.m. departure for Horsham. The crew seem to have forgotten the headcode discs.
(R. S. Greenwood)

PEASMARSH JUNCTION

This six inch to the mile map of 1920 shows the relationship of the junctions and the position of the embankment that might have carried SE & CR trains to Portsmouth, had not the LSWR acquired the Portsmouth Direct Line from its speculative builder.

7.8. These two views taken in 1924 show the former LSWR signal box at the junction of the Horsham line (on the left) and the Portsmouth line (under the bridge). Beyond the bridge can be seen Peasmarsh siding, which does not show on the map of 1912. The Horsham branch became single track in front of the LBSCR signal box which the Southern Railway eventually renamed Peasmarsh South to avoid having two boxes of the same name. In 1926 it was demolished, the single track then running up to the main line in which a crossover was inserted near the remaining signal box. (Late E. Wallis)

Table 38
GUILDFORD and HORSHAM

1953 timetable

9. The 7.55 from Horsham hauled by Class 2 tank No.41287 joining the main line on 25th May 1965 whilst the single line staff is received by the signalman. The train is about to use the crossover to the up line visible just beyond signal box. (John Scrace)

10.11. Tranquil scenes in peaceful
Edwardian days. (Lens of Sutton)

BRAMLEY

Station

_M P_

Church House

White House

Summerpool
House

Jolly Farmer (P.H.)

Pound

Trinity Church
(Vicarage)

Bramley

Post Office

12. Christmas shoppers were amongst the seven people killed during a German aerial attack on a passenger train that had just left Bramley station on 16th December 1942. A side corridor ran half the length of the coach and so no one was sitting near the windows. Greater injury would have occurred had it been a compartment coach.

This map of 1870 shows the only evidence we have found of the locomotive shed. It is probably the building on the right of the main line. The passing loop was not completed until 1876.

13. One of the long lasting M7 class accelerating away towards Guildford with three compartment coaches on 23rd June 1959. (S. C. Nash)

Fares from]	HORSHAM and GUILDFORD.—London, Brighton, and South Coast.													

Bradshaw's timetable for February 1890

"Good Lines" – The Monthly Journal of the
Commercial Travellers Christian Association

The level crossing and signal
box as seen in May 1965 (D. Osborne)

CRANLEIGH

15. An LBSCR train arrives from Horsham past the 18-lever signal box that was later moved to near where the cameraman is standing. Originally named Cranley, the spelling was changed in 1867 to avoid confusion at the Post office with Crawley. (Lens of Sutton)

17. Knowle Lane crossing as seen by the junior porter in 1923 when climbing to the top of the Down Home Signal to refill the oil lamp with paraffin, normally one of his weekly duties. (Late E. Wallis)

16. A platform snapshot on a sunny afternoon in Southern Railway days. (E. Jackson)

18. The top signal on the left was for starting trains to Guildford that had terminated at the station, whilst the smaller signal was for calling on trains for shunting only. This 1923 view shows the inevitable milk churns on the platform and an elderly horse box in the goods yard. (Late E. Wallis)

SOUTHERN RAILWAY.
Issued subject to the Bye-laws, Regulations &
Conditions in the Company's Bills and Notices.
H. M. F. on LEAVE
Cranleigh to
Cranleigh   Cranleigh
Waterloo   Waterloo
WATERLOO
Via Guildford
FIRST CLASS   FIRST CLASS
NOT TRANSFERABLE
0157   0157

20. Another Ramblers Excursion from Victoria, again double headed by goods engines, arrived on 2nd November 1952. They were Nos.30308 and 30693 of the 700 Class. The unusual square front to the leading wheel splashers contained sand for use on the wet rails. (S. C. Nash)

19. On 21st October 1951 a Ramblers Excursion ran from Victoria via Guildford and two C Class locomotives, Nos.31583 and 31576, are seen here pushing the empty coaches into the goods yard. The massive loading gantry can be seen in the background. Goods outward was notably timber whilst goods inward was biased towards coal, particularly for the gasworks which was at the end of the yard. (S. C. Nash)

21. Sunday 6th February 1955 the RCTS organised a railtour which included the Pulborough to Petersfield and Meon Valley lines on the day after their final passenger services had run. The train was double headed by two E5X Class 0-6-2 tank locomotives Nos.32570 and 32576 and is seen here near Cranleigh. The same train can be seen in our companion album "Branch Lines to Midhurst" arriving at Petersfield from Midhurst. (S. C. Nash)

CRANLEIGH

22. Two weeks before closure, the 18.05 from Guildford waits for the starting signal to be pulled off. These **BR Standard Class 2** tank locomotives handled most trains on the line in its final years. (J. Scrace)

23. This was the only passing place when the line opened and few changes ever occurred at this station, which was situated in Hogspudding Lane. An exception was the removal of the siding at the end of the platform ramp sometime after this 1923 view was taken. (Late E. Wallis)

BAYNARDS

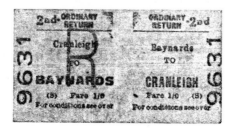

24. Baynards was a favourite location for film companies as its situation was so rural that no other buildings were visible. In February 1957 former LSWR Class T9 No.30310 and two coaches were used for the filming of "The Railway Children" for BBC TV. A later colour version was shot on the Keighley and Worth Valley Railway. The black mask over the locomotives number and crest are beginning to peel off! Class M7 No.30026 was used for most of the action shots. (S. C. Nash)

25. Signalman Geoff Birdfield is seen here opening the gates over the drive to Baynards Park in May 1965. The handwheel and mechanism had been removed to Bramley about 10 years earlier. The tunnel portal can be seen in the distance. (J. A. M. Vaughan)

26. Not only had he left the signal box to open the gates but he also had to man the booking office and then leave there to act as platform staff to see the train depart safely. All this interrupted the important work of preparing the famous dahlia beds, which had only proceeded as far as milepost 46. Since this was a former LBSCR line, distances were measured from Victoria, Waterloo being only 42 miles. (J. A. M. Vaughan)

27. Spot the goods clerk! Yes, Geoff Birdfield looked after the busy goods yard as well. It may not look busy with an empty wagon, a deserted goods shed and an idle 1-ton crane, but at the other end of the yard was a siding leading to the "earthworks". In early years it was a brickworks, later producing fullers earth for the woollen industry and, in more recent years, foundry clays. It also became a chemical processing works, and goods inward by rail included sulphur (400 tons annually from Italy via the Thames docks), tin ingots from Swansea, packaging from Sittingbourne, whilst goods outward ranged from seed dressings to polishing compounds. (Fox Photos)

28. Spot the signalman! Geoff Birdfield is working amongst his 1000 dahlia plants of 240 different varieties that he grew behind both platforms. Passing train crews acted as travelling salesmen along the line. (Fox Photos)

29. In the last years of operation the short morning working from Cranleigh to Guildford was extended to Baynards on Saturdays. It is seen here about to depart at 9.46 on 22nd May 1965 on the "wrong road" (J. Scrace)

30. The special train run by the LCGB on the day after public services ceased. These austerity Class QI's designed for freight work by Bulleid were introduced early in World War II. Although regarded as ugly by many, they were very good performers. (J. Scrace)

31. After closure, our friend with dahlia mania erected a 52 x 12 ft. glasshouse on the platform and cold frames on the track bed. This was the scene in 1972, two years after he had moved away. After 44 years railway service, he retired as a relief signalman in 1980. (J. A. M. Vaughan)

32. Baynards Tunnel was 381 yds long, always damp and on a gradient. A story is told of a QI Class locomotive climbing the hill with a long excursion train and slipping continuously in the tunnel, but in the dark and smoke the crew did not realise that the train had stopped and was running back, despite the fact that the locomotive was still working in forward gear. The white discs on the autotrain here indicate that this is the front of the train. The guard is restfully enjoying the view whilst the driver can just be seen above the window wiper.
(E. Gamblin/D. Wallis collection)

RUDGWICK

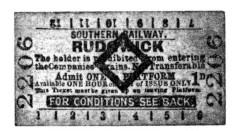

33. A view of an LBSCR train of 4-wheeled coaches to Horsham and the crowded goods yard with two horses waiting for their carts to be loaded. The wagon in the foreground is fitted with a tarpaulin hoop and the fifth wagon in has its initialled tarpaulin still in place. Notice also the loading gauge on the right and two signals on one post in the distance. (Lens of Sutton)

34. The daily goods is seen arriving from Guildford more than 50 years after the previous photograph was taken and little has changed except that a new upper quadrant signal, a new loading gauge and a larger signal box have arrived in new locations. The nearest wagon in the siding has been extended upwards for the carriage of coke and the farthest one is at an angle to the others because it has been on the small wagon turntable just visible. (Lens of Sutton)

35. Wagon turntables were widely used in the early years but this was the last to survive on the branch lines to Horsham, shown here in 1962. Wagons were moved by horse or by manpower aided by a pinch bar levered between the rail and one wheel. (R. A. Holder)

36. The prospective passenger's perspective on 23rd November 1957. In post war years many more boxes of mushrooms departed from this station than passengers. (J. Scrace Coll/Pamlin Prints)

38. Rudgwick station was built on a gradient of 1 in 80 but the Inspecting Officer of the Board of Trade refused to allow trains to stop on this incline. To alter the slope to the prescribed 1 in 130 it was necessary to raise the embankments and also the bridge over the River Arun. This was achieved by constructing a girder bridge above the original brick arch, creating an unusual structure never seen by the rail traveller. (J. Scrace)

←

37. Looking north under the B2128 roadbridge in 1964 when goods trains had ceased to use the head shunt on the right. (J. Scrace)

39. The 11.2 departure for Horsham on 13th April 1962 consists of an LMS designed 2-6-2 tank engine with two Maunsell designed coaches dating from the 1930s. The locomotive is displaying the additional equipment provided for autotrain working with push-pull units. (J. Scrace)

SLINFOLD

40. A quiet time between trains in the early part of this century, with an unaccompanied dog (for which there was a special fare) considering the virtues of Epps's Cocoa. (Lens of Sutton)

This map of 1876 shows two of three private sidings that once existed to serve a brickworks (later Duke & Ockendens) and timber yard (later Randalls ladders). These and the level crossing necessitated 3 signal boxes for many years.

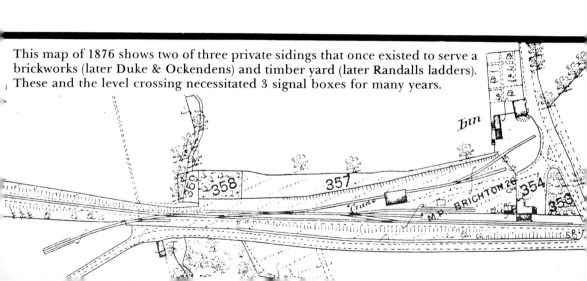

41. The staff and passenger pose oblivious to the unaccompanied dog and the elegant chimney on the unusual single storey extension to the station. (Lens of Sutton)

42. A former LBSCR Class E4 sets out towards Guildford about 1930 with the Westinghouse steam pump for the air brakes clearly visible on the cab side. The LSWR used vacuum brakes, thus the Southern Railway inherited a disagreeable mixture. (J. Scrace Coll.)

43. Every goods yard had a crane, even if only a small hand operated one like this. The sidings had gone when this picture was taken in July 1964. (J. Scrace)

CHRISTS HOSPITAL

44. The South Box is in the foreground and this view was taken from the top of its up home signal on 5th April 1923, with North Box just visible at the far end of the up platform. This station was opened in 1902 when the 'Bluecoat School' moved from London to spacious new premises nearby. The vast dimensions of the station were due to a large number of pupils being expected daily. In the event, the school governors decided that there would be boarders only thus defeating the railway's expectation of a large income to match the premises. The down loop was used principally by van trains containing the pupils luggage and their holiday specials. The Guildford branch platforms, complete with a footbridge, are on the left in the distance. (Late E. Wallis)

45. Signalman J. Mann poses at North Box on the same day. The previous box at this location was called Stammerham Junction. (Late E. Wallis)

46. We see here the changing of locomotives on a special train, circa 1939, in platform 5. No.1183 is a former SECR Class F1 "Jumbo". The fresh engine would be coupled to the other end of the train so the guard has the tail lamp ready, on the ground. (J. Scrace Coll.)

47. A Class M7 pulls the Brighton train away briskly at 1.43 p.m. on 3rd August 1953. The up electric from Bognor and Littlehampton, also due at 1.43, has just arrived, giving intending connecting passengers 1hr. 40mins. to enjoy the architectural delights of the junction station. (S. C. Nash)

48. The 9.02 Hove to Three Bridges arriving on 21st March 1959 behind Class C2X No.32529. In the foreground is the rusty conductor rail of the little used down loop and a close view of the point locking bar which prevents them being moved inadvertently under a passing train. (J. Scrace)

49. One of 20 Q Class goods locomotive designed by Maunsell and built in the late 1930's. The small cylinders of the steam reverses are visible above the centre driving wheels. The engine is proceeding towards Guildford 18th October 1964. (J. Scrace)

50. N Class locomotives were banned from this line. In this view one of them, No.31405, proceeds very slowly, as the cylinders are nearly touching the platform edge. It was there on the 12th March 1965 to take part in a film. By this time the footbridge had gone and passengers had to cross the branch line in front of 'A' Box (formerly North Box) if their train used platform 5. (J. Scrace)

51. The station was partly renamed for the filming of "Rotten to the Core" in which No.31405 appeared. (J. Scrace)

53. The fine exterior of the station, as seen here in 1968, survived the closure of the branch lines, but not for long. In 1972 a "funeral party" for 120 people was held by the staff and pupils of the nearby school on platform 2; the special ticket for it even had a black border. (J. Scrace)

52. Diesel hauled trains were very rare on this line. D.6572 is seen here leaving platform 4 at 16.58 for Guildford on 27th March 1965. The ground frame at this end of the platform had to be manned for the departure of every Guildford train. (J. Scrace)

54. Although electric trains still call here once an hour, only the subway and the platform 2 waiting room and toilet remain from the original buildings. Passengers from down trains no longer have to use the subway to leave the station, as the loop line has been filled in. (J. Scrace)

HORSHAM

55. A view taken in about 1865 looking south along the down platform and copied from an original hanging in the office of Station Master Hillier. (Late E. Wallis Coll.)

57. A Class C3 No.307 shunting circa 1924. The large building was called the 'tranship shed' where goods to and from local stations were transhipped to make up full loads. The door of an open wagon had been left down on the platform in the shed one night when the pilot engine came in and coupled up. It not only pulled out the wagons, but most of the end of the shed at the same time (Late E. Wallis)

56. A similar view taken on 21st June, 1925, showing the replacement canopy and West Box. (Late E. Wallis)

58. The Junction Box and inner home signals around 1910, with the locomotive round house behind. (Late E. Wallis Coll.)

59. There were three boxes working simultaneously for many years. Signalman Jesse Jupp, himself a competent photographer is pictured here on 11th August 1924. This box was situated on the north end of the down platform.
(Late E. Wallis)

60. Frank Holmes joined the LBSCR at the age of 14 and is seen here inside the Junction Box, where he had to record every movement in the train register. More recently, he was well known locally as a J.P. (F. Holmes Coll.)

This 1876 map shows the earlier position of the locomotive shed and turntable, plus numerous wagon turntables.

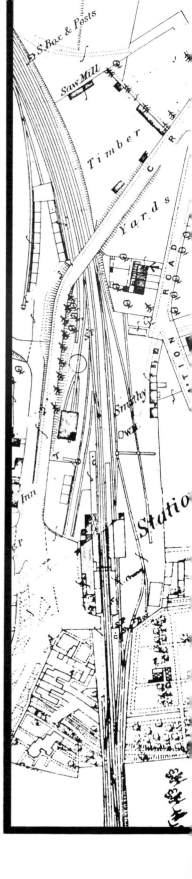

61. The West Box received some temporary bracing during repairs in 1928.
(Late E. Wallis)

62. Signalman Hooper on duty in West Box whilst the stilts were being repaired.
(Late E. Wallis)

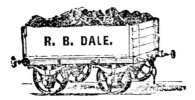

63. The locomotive round house and water tank in about 1922 with (from left to right) Class D1, B1 and C3 engines. The replacement turntable frame was waiting to be fitted, so that the new heavy Moguls could be turned. (Late E. Wallis)

"Good Lines" – The Monthly Journal of the
Commercial Travellers Christian Association

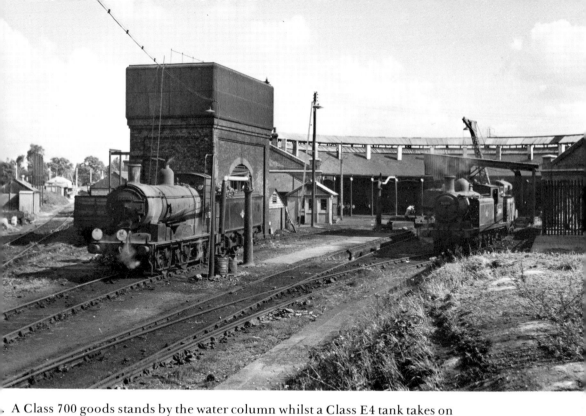

A Class 700 goods stands by the water column whilst a Class E4 tank takes on coal, on 30th August 1959. The coaling stage was originally behind the water tower. (J. Scrace)

One of the last of the elderly Class D3 locomotives awaiting servicing on 23rd August 1952. Built in 1893, it ran over 1.5 million miles before withdrawal in April 1953. (R. G. Jarvis)

These events are self explanatory. Horsham teams have won an impressive number of awards over many years.

66. From left to right –
H. Pollitt (Loco. Supt.),
unknown member,
L. Gorringe,
Nobby Worcester,
L. Weller,
E. Clack,
W. Luxford and
Dr. Clement Cooke.
(F. Holmes Coll.) 1926

68. This aerial view,
taken in 1958, shows
the position of the all
electric signal box
which replaced the
three mechanical
ones. It is located
between the junction
and the roundhouse.
(R. G. Spalding/
Meridian Airmaps
Ltd.)

67. Team members
from left to right –
W. E. Jupp (Captain),
A. Hickman,
A. Binstead,
A. Player and
J. Scrace.
(British Rail) 1960

70. A northward view of a branch line train in 1937 during the reconstruction of the station, which provided four through platforms for the first time. (E. Jackson)

69. A German bomb landed on the main line south of Horsham on 7th October 1940 and C2X Class No.2550 ran into the crater.

71. Electric trains started to use the new station on 2nd July 1938 and here we see a second generation electric set on the 17.02 service from Victoria on 22nd April 1964. The 18.26 train for Brighton is still in the carriage siding. Colour light signals were introduced at 12.5 a.m. on 24th April 1938 but the new platforms were surprisingly illuminated by gaslight. (J. Scrace)

72. 73. The exterior as seen in the 1930s above, and the replacement station in the 1970s below. (E. Jackson and J. Scrace)

ITCHINGFIELD JUNCTION

74. Looking south, the Steyning line is seen branching to the left from the main line to Portsmouth, around 1923. (Late E. Wallis)

75. The position of this signal box is shown on the map overleaf. The picture was taken in 1920 by Mr. Steptoe just before it was demolished. (Late E. Wallis Coll.)

76. Signalman T. Boorman poses in front of his box on 26th March 1923. It was of unusual design because it had an internal staircase. Bromley Junction Norwood was probably the only other one on the LBSCR to have this feature.
(Late E. Wallis)

78. After 3rd May, 1964, passenger services were operated by diesel-electric multiple unit sets of a type seen here passing Junction Cottages on 27th March 1965. (J. Scrace)

Map of 1897. The siding shown was for agricultural traffic and was removed when Christs Hospital station was opened in 1902. At the same time the level crossing was replaced by an overbridge for the Barns Green Road.

77. On 5th March 1964 there was a serious collision between two freight trains. The 01.50 Brighton to Three Bridges freight had been diverted to run via Henfield due to engineering works on the main line and, having run past adverse signals, collided with the 02.30 Three Bridges to Chichester hitting it at about the nineteenth wagon, the latter train being composed of about 65 trucks. The crew of the 01.50's engine, D6502, were killed. It was the opinion of many railwaymen that the crew of the Brighton train had been sent to sleep by the combined effects of poor ventilation and fumes in the diesel's cab. This view shows it being cut up on site 17 days after the accident; the first of its class to be withdrawn. (J. Scrace)

Siding Cottages

P

S.P.

S.Ps.

Signal Box

Junctio Cottage

79. A typical LBSCR country station. Notice the well covered solitary lady passenger, the wooden hand crane, the chimney of the brickworks, the siding leading to it, the horse box and inevitable milk churn.
(Lens of Sutton)

SOUTH - WATER

80. By 1924 the brickworks had two chimneys. This was the only station on the line without a footbridge, passengers having to use the crossing in the foreground.
(Late E. Wallis)

81. This aerial view, taken in 1958, shows the extent of the brickworks and its narrow gauge railway. Only a few coal wagons are visible, whereas in earlier days there would have been many more, with even more brick wagons waiting for despatch. The road over the railway was the A24 between London and Worthing. (R. G. Spalding/ Meridian Airmaps Ltd.)

SOUTHWATER STATION

82. Class C2X No.32527 plods along with a mixed freight from Hove to Three Bridges on 14th March 1959. The extra dome was not for sand, which was common in mainland Europe, but once covered a top feed water valve. The replacement clack valve can be seen below it. The four assorted ageing horse boxes were coupled behind the engine, rather than elsewhere in the train, to improve the braking of the train, as they were fitted with vacuum brakes unlike the following open wagons. (John Scrace)

83. Looking north in 1964 we see, from left to right, the tiny goods shed, the cattle pen, the former station master's house (now a private residence), beyond which were the main station buildings (now a store for the local horticultural society), the A24 bridge, six elegant oil lampposts on the down side and an SR signal post made from two old rails. (J. Scrace)

WEST GRINSTEAD

84. A mystery view, reputed to be circa 1865. If it was taken before the line was doubled, why are there two smoke marks on the bridge? Were the sleeper marks in the ballast made by the contractor's temporary way? (Late E. Wallis Coll.)

85. The down platform shelter on the left is nearly 20 years younger than its dissimilar counterpart opposite, which sufficed whilst the line was only a single track. The main station buildings, high up on the right, are at road level, the road now being the A272. (Late E. Wallis)

86 Looking north towards the white painted cattle pen, we also see the liberal use of wagon tarpaulins. Both views were taken in 1924. (Late E. Wallis)

88. The family of the station master (Mr. Bartlett) are the only passengers alighting from the 13.30 Brighton to Horsham on 30th April 1964. A smart set of Bulleid's coaches compliment a reasonably clean Class 2 Tank. (J. Scrace)

87. By the time this photograph was taken in 1955 all that remains of the original up platform shelter is the brick wall. Its successor matches its opposite number quite well, apart from the lack of canopy valancing. Note the carefully shaped smoke deflectors under the lattice footbridge. (J. Aston)

PARTRIDGE GREEN

89. An undated early northward view, when country stations were the centre of activity. (Lens of Sutton)

90. Beyond the up platform shelter are a row of cottages thought to have been erected for the line's construction workers. (Lens of Sutton)

91. Looking south with Class C2X No.32522 arriving with a short freight train in 1960. The goods shed is seen beyond the station-master's house. (P. Hay)

HENFIELD

92. Class D3 No.392 named "Polegate" stands on the wrong road for reasons unknown. It wa built at Brighton to the design of R. Billinton in 1894 and withdrawn from service in 1933 (R. G. Spalding Coll.)

93. The crew of a Brighton bound train pose for an unknown photographer in LBSCR day (J. Scrace Coll.)

4. A motor train from Brighton passes the goods yard on the same day with push-pull set No.716 built in 1921, propelled by another M7, BR No.30053. "Smoking" was indelibly etched in large letters onto the windows of the leading coach whilst "No Smoking" appeared only on the next three compartments, printed on small stickers, easily removed by those with contrary views. (P. Hay)

5. Formerly LSWR Class M7 No.47 accelerates past the goods shed in October 1957, displaying its rhythmically hissing brake pump. (P. Hay)

HENFIELD

96. The scene at 1.15 a.m. on the Sunday morning after the passengers had left. Waiting room furniture is being loaded across the down line into a van train hauled by D.6568. (J. W. Whiting)

97. In the autumn of 1966 the PW huts were loaded by steam crane prior to track lifting. (J. W. Whiting)

STEYNING

8. The goods yard on market day. The difference between the horse box, with its groom compartment, and the relatively open cattle wagon can be seen. This photograph was taken about 1925 by Mr. Bernard Holden who was to spend much of his railway career on the Steyning line. At that time he lived in the station house as his Father was Station Master. He is now writing a detailed history of the line and is well known as Superintendent of the Bluebell Railway.

9. Built at Brighton by the LBSCR as No.86 at a cost of £2649 in September, 1912, this member of the I3 Class is seen here taking water from the down platform column. Below the buffer beam is a typical LBSCR ground signal, the head of which rotated after the points were reset. (Lens of Sutton)

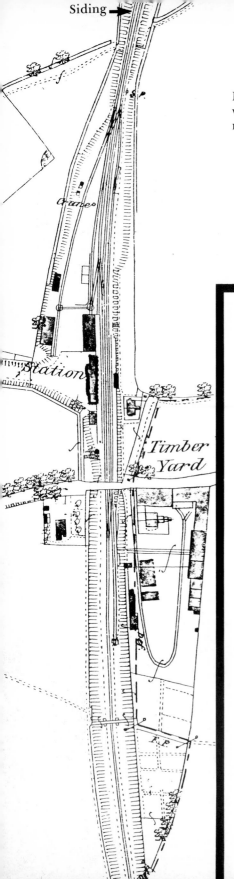

Map of 1875, before doubling of the main line, showing wagon turntables in the goods yard and a narrow gauge railway in the timber yard.

It is difficult to imagine the enthusiasm of ramblers when reading the following report in a Southern Railway publication – "The last time I began a walk from Steyning Station was at midnight in mid-summer to see the moon set and the sun rise. On that occasion I was not alone. There were in all 1330 fellow wayfarers equally ready to take this double risk. We enjoyed ourselves hugely, but we saw neither the down setting of the one nor the uprising of the other. We experienced a chilly, damp dawn that made enjoyment a matter of determination rather than instinct". The return train was from Amberley! (N. C. Langridge Coll.)

100. The final design of push-pull set stands in the down platform in July, 1960. The massive water tank on the left was filled in the early days by a steam operated pump situated behind the elegant round-headed doorway. There was also a tall factory-like chimney alongside. (R. A. Holder)

101. The fine symmetry of the exterior was slightly marred in later years by the little porch and telephone kiosk, but who cared providing they were functional? It matters not now, as only the goods shed survived the construction of the bypass. (Lens of Sutton)

102. 103. The Centenary of the line was celebrated on 7th October, 1961, with a special train hauled by E4 Class No.32468, bunting, banners, and a visit by the Brighton Works shunter. This is the locomotive attracting the crowds by the goods shed, a Terrier built in 1872 at Brighton and withdrawn in 1963, being sold the following year to the Bluebell Railway, who restored its original name of Fenchurch. (R. Holder) (S. C. Nash)

104. The 6.13 ex-Brighton accelerates past the disused goods
yard on 12th June 1963 (S. C. Nash)

London Brighton and South
Coast Railway.

Partridge Green to

Baynards

BRAMBER

106. The view north-wards from the foot-bridge in April, 1925, showing the Steyning Up Distant signal. Bramber signal box was closed in 1910. (Late E. Wallis)

105. This aerial view in 1958 shows two road bridges. The northern or bypass bridge was built at the start of World War II to allow the passage of tanks, which the original bridge could not sup-port. The plans for a "Tank Bridge" were dated 7.11.38 which re-veals the local distrust of the Munich Agreement which was signed on 29.9.38. All road traffic was diverted over the wartime bridge in the 1960s and plans were drawn for a concrete bridge to replace the two, but closure of the railway meant that the Steyning and Bramber bypass could be built on the trackbed. A roundabout is now on the site of the former bridges.
(R. G. Spalding/ Meridian Airmaps Ltd.)

107. Looking towards the South Downs in the dusk. The locomotive is a former SECR H Class tank, seen here pushing three coaches towards Brighton on 25th August, 1960. This was the only station south of Hor-sham on this branch to be electrically lit.
(R. A. Holder)

GENTLEMEN

108. The guard of a northbound train of assorted coaches appears to wait patiently whilst the loco crew and station staff carry out a private transaction.

109. Another Class 2 tank engine, very common in the last years of steam on the line, runs in with a southbound train. Both views were taken in the summer of 1960 by C. R. L. Coles.

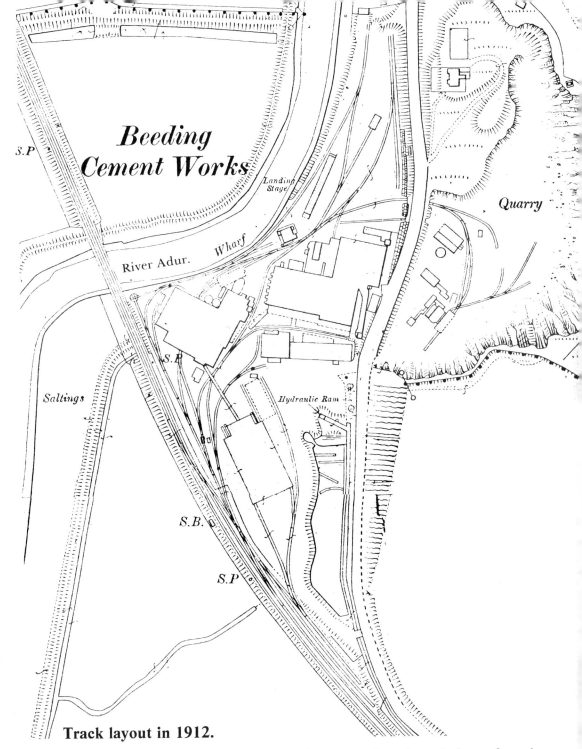

Beeding
Cement Works

Landing Stage

Quarry

River Adur. Wharf

S.P

S.P

Saltings

Hydraulic Ram

S.B.

S.P

Track layout in 1912.

Clay is an important ingredient in the manufacture of cement and was brought by sea from the Medway until 1896, when the Sussex Portland Cement Co. installed sidings so that the LBSCR could transport it from Newhaven. About 1902 this traffic ceased, the clay then being brought down the river by barge from Horton. After a few years steam wagons were introduced which in turn were displaced by a pipeline in 1950. In addition to vast quantities of coal arriving by rail, gypsum was transported from Mountfield in East Sussex, the last load coming on 21st April 1980.

110. The position of Beeding Sidings signal box can be seen on the map and in the aerial photograph. (D. Cullum Coll.)

111. Aerial view of the new works taken in 1958.
(R. G. Spalding/Meridian Airmaps Ltd)

12. The present works was completed in 1951 and was provided with modern rail facilities including a tippler for mineral wagons. (Blue Circle Industries)

13. A long day out. An excursion from Peterborough to Hove passes through the Adur Gap on 7th June, 1956. The train is composed of Class UI No.31904, West Country Class No.34047 and a mixture of pre-war LNER coaches. (P. Hay)

114. Cement works traffic over the remaining single line was once daily, but this dwindled leading to complete closure in 1981. Here a Class 73 electro-diesel follows the River Adur on 13th April 1971. (J. A. M. Vaughan)

115. Track lifting outside the cement works near the River Adur bridge in October 1966. (J. Whiting)

116. Two railwaymen were necessary at busy times to collect the bridge tolls on the level crossing, as is evident in this picture taken on 12th May, 1963. (D. Osborne)

117. On 13th June, 1965, Battle of Britain Class 4-6-2 "Royal Observer Corps." hauled the LCGB's railtour "The Wealdsman", seen here leaving Shoreham. (J. A. M. Vaughan)

←

118. Looking north wards in April, 1967, with the cement works visible beyond the new road bridge. (J. A. M. Vaughan)

119. On the same day Class 73 No. E6025 pulls away from the 1740 trestle bridge, the toll right of which the railway acquired when the line was opened, as a result of a complicated deal with the Duke of Norfolk who owned both bridges at Shoreham at that time. (J. A. M. Vaughan)

120. A LSWR Class M7 from the turn of the century hauls an SECR brake 3rd from 1920, an LBSCR auto trailer from 1914 and an SR van in BR days. The train has just left Shoreham station on the electrified coast line and will pass milepost 6 before turning onto the Steyning line. (P. Hay)

SHOREHAM

121. A scene on the last day that it was possible to call at all stations to Horsham – May 5th 1966. (J. A. M. Vaughan)

122. Horsham trains usually used platform 3 at Brighton. Here we see Class D3 No.32379 leaving with a former LBSCR 2-coach motor set in 1951. The old tender on the left was used for carrying sludge from the locomotive water treatment plant whilst in the background there is the elegant Pullman car "Rita". (P. Hay)

BRIGHTON

123. A Class E4 runs over the complicated trackwork on its way to Horsham on 8th September 1960. Part of the locomotive works, where many of the engines we have seen in this album were built, is visible on the left. (J. Scrace)